SWARAJ IN ONE YEAR

MAHATMA GANDHI

AMS PRESS
NEW YORK

SWARAJ IN ONE YEAR

MAHATMA GANDHI

2nd EDITION

PUBLISHERS :
GANESH & CO., MADRAS
1921

Library of Congress Cataloging in Publication Data

Gandhi, Mohandas Karamchand, 1869-1948.
    Swaraj in one year.

    Reprint of the 1921 ed.
    1. India--Politics and government--1919-1947.
I. Title.
DS480.45.G298   1972   320.9'54   75-168095
ISBN 0-404-02676-1

Reprinted from the edition of 1921, Madras
First AMS edition published in 1972
Manufactured in the United States of America

International Standard Book Number: 0-404-02676-1

AMS PRESS INC.
NEW YORK, N. Y.   10003

CONTENTS

SWARAJ IN ONE YEAR

*[In moving the resolution on non-co-operation
at the special sessions of the Indian
National Congress held at Calcutta in
September, 1920, Mr. Gandhi spoke as
follows:—]*

I am aware, more than aware, of the
grave responsibility that rests on my shoulders in being privileged to move this resolution
before this great assembly. I am aware that
my difficulties, as also yours, increase if you
are able to adopt this resolution. I am also
aware that the adoption of any resolution will
mark a definite change in the policy which
the country has hitherto adopted for the
vindication of the rights that belong to it,
and its honour. I am aware that a large
number of our leaders who have given the
time and attention to the affairs of my motherland, which I have not been able to give, are
ranged against me. They think it a duty to
resist the policy revolutionising the Government policy at any cost. Knowing this I
stand before you in fear of God and a sense

of duty to put this before you for your hearty acceptance.

I ask you to dismiss me, for the time being, from your consideration. I have been charged of saintliness and a desire for dictatorship. I venture to say that I do not stand before you either as a saint or a candidate for dictatorship. I stand before you to present to you the results of my many years' practical experience in non-co-operation. I deny the charge that it is a new thing in the country. It has been accepted at hundreds of meetings attended by thousands of men, and has been placed in working order since the first of August by the Mussalmans, and many of the things in the programme are being enforced in a more or less intense form. I ask you again to dismiss personalities in the consideration of this important question, and bring to bear patient and calm judgment on it. But a mere acceptance of the resolution does not end the work. Every individual has to enforce the items of the resolution in so far as they apply to him. I beseech you to give me a patient hearing. I ask you neither to clap nor to hiss. I do not mind them so far as I am concerned, but clapping hinders the flow of thought, clapping and hissing hinder the process of correspondence between a speaker and his audience. You will not hiss out of the stage any single speaker. For non-co-operation is a measure of discipline and sacrifice and it demands patience and respect for opposite views. And unless we were able to evolve a spirit of mutual toleration for diametrically opposite views, non-co-operation is an impossibility. Non-co-operation in an angry atmosphere is an impossibility. I have learnt through bitter experience the one supreme lesson to conserve my anger, and as heat conserved is transmuted into energy, even so our anger controlled can be transmuted into a power which can move the world. To those who have been attending the Congress, as brothers in arms I ask what can be better discipline than that, which we should exercise between ourselves.

I have been told that I have been doing nothing but wreckage and that by bringing forward the resolution, I am breaking up the political life of the country. The Congress is not a party organisation. It ought to provide a platform for all shades of opinions, and a minority need not leave this organisation, but

may look forward to translate itself into a
majority, in course of time, if its opinion
commended itself to the country. Only let no
man in the name of the Congress advocate a
policy which has been condemned by the
Congress. And if you condemn my policy I
shall not go away from the Congress, but shall
plead with them to convert the minority into
a majority.

There are no two opinions as to the wrong
done to the Khilafat. Mussalmans cannot
remain as honourable men and follow their
Prophet if they do not vindicate their honour
at any cost. The Punjab has been cruelly,
brutally treated, and inasmuch as one man in
the Punjab was made to crawl on his belly the
whole of India crawled on her belly, and if
we are worthy sons and daughters of India we
should be pledged to remove these wrongs. It
is in order to remove these wrongs that the
country is agitating itself. But we have not
been able to bend the Government to our will.
We cannot rest satisfied with a mere expression
of angry feeling. You could not have heard a
more passionate denunciation of the Punjab
wrongs than in the pages of the presidential
address. If the Congress cannot wring justice

from unwilling hands how can it vindicate its existence and its honour? How can it do so if it cannot enforce clear repentence, before receiving a single gift, however rich, from those bloodstained hands.

I have therefore placed before you my scheme of non-co-operation to achieve this end and want you to reject any other scheme, unless you have deliberately come to the conclusion that it is a better scheme than mine. If there is a sufficient response to my scheme I make bold to reiterate my statement that you can gain Swarajya in the course of an year. Not the passing of the resolution will bring Swarajya, but the enforcement of the resolution from day to day in a progressive manner, due regard being had to the conditions in the country. There is another remedy before the country, and that is drawing of the sword. If that was possible India would not have listened to the gospel of non-co-operation. I want to suggest to you that even if you want to arrest injustice by methods of violence, discipline and self-sacrifice are necessary. I have not known of a war gained by a rabble, but I have known of wars gained by disciplined armies, and if you want to give battle to the British Government and to the combined power of Europe we must train ourselves in discipline and self-sacrifice. I confess I have become impatient. I have seen that we deserve Swarajya to-day, but we have not got the spirit of national sacrifice. We have evolved this spirit in domestic affairs, and I have come to ask you to extend it to other affairs. I have been travelling from one end to the other of the country to see whether the country has evolved the national spirit, whether at the alter of the nation it is ready to dedicate its riches, children, its all if it was ready to make the initiatory sacrifice. Is the country ready? Are the title-holders ready to surrender their titles? Are parents ready to sacrifice literary education of their children for the sake of the country? The schools and colleges are really a factory for turning out clerks for Government. If the parents are not ready for the sacrifice, if title-holders not ready, Swarajya is very nearly an impossibility. No nation being under another nation can accept gifts and kicks at the responsibility attaching to those gifts, imposed by the conquering nation. Immediately the conquered

country realised instinctively that any gift
which might come to it is not for the benefit
of the conquered, but for the benefit of the
conqueror, that moment it should reject every
form of voluntary assistance to him. These
are the fundamental essentials of success in
the struggle for the independence for the
country, whether within the Empire or without
the Empire. I hold a real substantial unity
between Hindus and Musalmans infinitely
superior to the British connection and if
I had to make a choice between that unity and
the British connection, I would have the
first and reject the other. If I had to choose
between the honour of the Punjab, anarchy,
neglect of education, shutting out of all legislative activity and British connection, I
would choose the honour of the Punjab and
all it meant, even anarchy, shutting out of all
schools, etc. without slightest hesitation.

   If you have the same feeling burning in
you as in me for the honour of Islam and the
Punjab then you will unreservedly accept my
resolution.

   I now come to the burning topic, *viz.*, the
boycott of the councils. Sharpest difference
of opinion existed regarding this and if the

house has to divide on it, it must divide on one issue, *viz.*, whether Swarajya has to be gained through the councils or without the councils. If we utterly distrust the British Government and we know that they are utterly unrepentant how can you believe that the councils will lead to Swarajya and not tighten the British hold on India?

I now come to Swadeshi. The boycott of foreign goods is included in the resolution. You have got here, I confess, an anomaly for which I am not originally responsible. But I have consented to it. I will not go into the history of how it found a place into the resolution, of which the essence is discipline and self-sacrifice. Swadeshi means permanent boycott of foreign goods. It is therefore a matter of redundancy. But I have taken it in, because I could not reject it as a matter of conscience. I know, however, it is a physical inpossibility. So long as we have to rely on the pins and needles—figurative and literal both—we cannot bring about a complete boycott of foreign goods. I do not hesitate to say this clause mars the musical harmony, if I may claim it without vanity, of the programme. I feel that those words do mar the symmetry of

the programme. But I am not here for symmetry of the programme as for its workability.

I again ask you not to be influenced by
personality. Reject out of your consideration
any service that I have done. Two things
only I claim. Laborious industry, great
thought behind any programme and unflinch-
ing determination to bring it about. You may
take only those things from me, and bring
them to bear on any programme that you
adopt.

THE NON-CO-OPERATION RESOLUTION.

In view of the fact that on the Khilafat
question both the Indian and Imperial Governments have signally failed in their duty towards
the Musalmans of India, and the Prime Minister
has deliberately broken his pledged word given
to them, and that it is the duty of every non-
Moslem Indian in every legitimate manner to
assist his Musalman brother in this attempt to
remove the religious calamity that has overtaken him :

And in view of the fact that in the matter
of the events of the April of 1919 both the said
Governments have grossly neglected or failed
to protect the innocent people of the Puujab

and punish officers guilty of unsoldierly and
barbarous behaviour towards them and have
exonerated Sir Michael O'Dwyer who proved
himself directly or indirectly responsible for the
most of the official crimes and callous to the
sufferings of the people placed under his
administration, and that the debate in the
House of Lords betrayed a woeful lack of
sympathy with the people of India and showed
virtual support of the systematic terrorism and
frightfulness adopted in the Punjab and that
the latest Viceregal pronouncement is proof of
entire absence of repentance in the matters of
the Khilafat and the Punjab :

This Congress is of opinion that there can
be no contentment in India without redress of
the two aforementioned wrongs, and that the
only effectual means to vindicate national
honour and to prevent a repetition of similar
wrongs in future is the establishment of Swarajya. This Congress is further of opinion that
there is no course left open for the people of
India but to approve of and adopt the policy of
progressive non-violent non-co-operation until
the said wrongs are righted and Swarajya is
established.

And in as much as a beginning should be made by the classes who have hitherto moulded and represénted opinion and in as much as Government consolidates its power through titles and honours bestowed on the people, through schools controlled by it, its law courts and its legislative councils, and in as much as it is desirable in the prosecution of the movement to take the minimum risk and to call for the least sacrifice compatible with the attainment of the desired object, this Congress earnestly advises—

(*a*) surrender of titles and honorary offices and resignation from nominated seats in local bodies ;

(*b*) refusal to attend Government Levees, Durbars and other official and semi-official functions held by Government officials or in their honour ;

(*c*) gradual withdrawal of children from Schools and Colleges owned, aided or controlled by Government and in place of such schools and colleges establishment of National Schools and Colleges in the various Provinces ;

(*d*) gradual boycott of British Courts by lawyers and litigants and establishment of private arbitration courts by their aid for the settlement of private disputes;

(e) refusal on the part of the military, clerical and labouring classes to offer themselves as recruits for service in Mesopotamia;

(f) withdrawal by candidates of their candidature for election to the Reformed Councils and refusal on the part of the voters to vote for any candidate who may despite the Congress advice offer himself for election; and

(g) the boycott of foreign goods.

And in as much as non-co-operation has been conceived as a measure of discipline and self-sacrifice without which no nation can make real progress, and in as much as an opportunity should be given in the very first stage of non-co-operation to every man, woman and child, for such discipline and self-sacrifice, this Congress advices adoption of Swadeshi in piece-goods on a vast scale, and in as much as the existing mills of India with indigenous capital and control do not manufacture sufficient yarn and sufficient cloth for the requirements of the nation, and are not likely to do so for a long time to come, this Congress advises immediate stimulation of further manufacture on a large scale by means of reviving hand-spinning in every home and hand-weaving on the part of the millions of weavers who have abandoned their ancient and honourable calling for want of encouragement.

SWARAJ IN ONE YEAR

Much laughter has been indulged in at my expense for having told the Congress audience at Calcutta that if there was sufficient response to my programme of non-co-operation Swaraj would be attained in one year. Some have ignored my condition and laughed because of the impossibility of getting Swaraj anyhow within one year. Others have spelt the 'if' in capitals and suggested that if 'ifs' were permissible in argument, any absurdity could be proved to be a possibility. My proposition however is based on a mathematical calculation. And I venture to say that true Swaraj is a practical impossibility without due fulfilment of my conditions. Swaraj means a state such that we can maintain our separate existence without the presence of the English. If it is to be a partnership, it must be a partnership at will. There can be no Swaraj without our feeling and being the equals of Englishmen. To-day we feel that we are dependent upon them for our internal and external security, for an armed peace between the Hindus and the Musalmans, for our education and for the supply of daily wants, nay, even for the settlement of our religious squabbles. The Rajahs are dependant upon the British for their powers and millionaires for their millions. The British know our helplessness and Sir Thomas Holland cracks jokes quite legitimately at the expense of non-co-operationists. To get Swaraj then is to get rid of our helplessness. The problem is no doubt stupendous even as it is for the fabled lion who having been brought up in the company of goats found it impossible to feel that he was a lion. As Tolstoy used to put it, mankind often laboured under hypnotism. Under its spell continuously we feel the feeling of helplessness. The British themselves cannot be expected to help us out of it. On the contrary, they din into our ears that we shall be fit to govern ourselves only by slow educative processes. The " *Times* " suggested that if we boycott the councils we shall lose the opportunity of a training in Swaraj. I have no doubt that there are many who believe what the " *Times* " says. It even resorts to a falsehood. It audaciously says that Lord Milner's Mission listened to the

Egyptians only when they were ready to lift
the boycott of the Egyptian Council. For me
the only training in Swaraj we need is the
ability to defend ourselves against the whole
world and to live our natural life in perfect freedom even though it may be full of defects.
Good government is no substitute for self-
government. The Afghans have a bad government but it is self-government. I envy them.
The Japanese learnt the art through a sea of
blood. And if we to-day had the power to drive
out the English by superior brute-force, we
would be counted their superiors, and in spite
of our inexperience in debating at the Council
table or in holding executive offices, we
would be held fit to govern ourselves.
For brute-force is the only test the West has
hitherto recognised. The Germans were defeat-
ed not because they were necessarily in the
wrong, but because the allied Powers were found
to possess greater brute strength. In the end
therefore India must either learn the art of war
which the British will not teach her or she
must follow her own way of discipline and self-
sacrifice through non-co-operation. It is as
amazing as it is humiliating that less than one
hundred thousand white men should be able to

rule three hundred and fifteen million Indians. They do so somewhat undoubtedly by force but more by securing our co-operation in a thousand ways and making us more and more helpless and dependent on them as time goes forward. Let us not mistake reformed councils more law-courts and even governor-ships for real freedom or power. They are but subtler methods of emasculation. The British cannot rule us by mere force. And so they resort to all means, honourable and dishonour-able, in order to retain their hold on India. They want India's billions and they want India's man power for their imperialistic greed. If we refuse to supply them with men and money, we achieve our goal, namely, Swaraj, equality, manliness.

The cup of our humiliation was filled during the closing scenes in the Viceregal council. Mr. Shastri could not move his resolution on the Punjab. The Indian victims of Jallianwalla received Rs. 1,250, the English victims of mobfrenzy received lacs. The officials who were guilty of crimes against those whose servants they were, were repri-manded. And the councillors were satisfied. If India were powerful, India would not

2

have stood this addition of insult to her injury.

I do not blame the British. If we were weak in numbers as they are, we too would perhaps have resorted to the same methods as they are now employing. Terrorism and deception are weapons not of the strong but of the weak. The British are weak in numbers, we are weak in spite of our numbers. The result is that each is dragging the other down. It is common experience that Englishmen lose in character after residence in India, and that Indians lose in courage and manliness by contact with Englishmen. This process of weakening is good neither for us, two nations, nor for the world.

But if we Indians take care of ourselves the English and the rest of the world would take care of themselves. Our contribution to the world's progress must therefore consist in setting our own house in order.

Training in arms for the present is out of the question. I go a step further and believe that India has a better mission for the world. It is within her power to show that she can achieve her destiny by pure self-sacrifice, *i.e.*, self-purification. This can be done only by non-co-operation. And non-co-operation is possible only when those who commenced to co-operate begin the process of withdrawal. If we can but free ourselves from the threefold *maya* of Government controlled schools, Government law-courts and legislative councils, and truly control our own education, regulate our disputes and be indifferent to their legislation, we are ready to govern ourselves, and we are only then ready to ask Government servants, whether civil or military, to resign, and the ta-xpayers to suspend payment of taxes.

And is it such an impracticable proposition to expect parents to withdraw their children from schools and' colleges and establish their own institutions or to ask lawyers to suspend their practice and devote their whole time and attention to national service against payment, where necessary, of their main-tenance, or to ask candidates for councils not to enter councils and lend their passive or active assistance to the legislative machinery through which all control is exercised. The movement of non-co-operation is nothing but an attempt to isolate the brute-force of the British from all the trappings under which it is hidden and to show that brute-force by itself cannot, for one single moment, hold India.

But I frankly confess that, until the three conditions mentioned by me are fulfilled, there is no Swaraj. We may not go on taking our college degrees, taking thousands of rupees monthly from clients for cases which can be finished in five minutes and taking the keenest delight in wasting national time on the council floor and still expect to gain national self-respect.

The last though not the least important part of the *Maya* still remains to be considered. That is Swadeshi. Had we not abandoned Swadeshi, we need not have been in the present fallen state. If we would get rid of the economic slavery, we must manufacture our own cloth and at the present moment only by hand-spinning and hand weaving.

All this means discipline, self-denial, self-sacrifice, organising ability, confidence and courage. If we show this in one year among the classes that to-day count, and make public opinion, certainly gain Swaraj within a one year. If I am told that even we who lead have not these qualities in us, there certainly will never be Swaraj for India, but then we shall have no right to blame the English for what they are doing.   Our salvation and its time are solely dependent upon us.

Young India—September 22, 1920.

SWARAJ IN NINE MONTHS

Asked by the *Times* representative as to his impressions formed as a result of his activities during the last three months, Mr. Gandhi said :—" My own impression of these three months' extensive experience is that this movement of non-co-operation has come to stay, and it is most decidedly a purifying movement, in spite of isolated instances of rowdyism, as for instance at Mrs. Besant's meeting in Bombay, at some places in Delhi, Bengal and even in Gujarat. The people are assimilating day after day the spirit of non-violence, not necessarily as a creed, but as an inevitable policy. I expect most startling results, more startling than, say, the discoveries of Sir J. C. Bose, or the acceptance by the people of non-violence. If the Government could be assured beyond any possibility of doubt that no violence would ever be offered by us the Government would from that moment alter its character, unconsciously and involuntarily, but none the less surely on that account."

" Alter its character,—in what directions ?" asked the *Times* representative.

" Certainly in the direction which we ask it should move—that being in the direction of Government becoming responsive to every call of the nation."

" Will you kindly explain further ?" asked our representative.

" By that I mean," said Mr. Gandhi, " people will be able by asserting themselves through fixed determination and self-sacrifice to gain the redress of the Khilafat wrong, the Punjab wrong, and attain the Swaraj of their choice."

" But what is .your Swaraj, and where does the Government come in there—the Government which you say will alter its character unconsciously ?"

" My Swaraj," said Mr. Gandhi, " is the Parliamentary government of India in the modern sense of the term for the time being, and that government would be secured to us either through the friendly offices of the British people or without them."

" What do you mean by the phrase, ' without them !' " questioned the interviewer.

"This moment," continued Mr. Gandhi, "is an endeavour to purge the present Government of selfishness and greed which determine almost every one of their activities. Suppose that we have made it impossible by disassociation from them to feed their greed. They might not wish to remain in India, as happened in the case of Somaliland, where the moment its administration ceased to be a paying proposition they evacuated it."

"How do you think," queried the representative, "in practice this will work out?"

"What I have sketched before you," said Mr. Gandhi, "is the final possibility. What I expect is that nothing of that kind will happen. In so far as I understand the British people they will recognise the force of public opinion when it has become real and patent. Then, and only then, will they realise the hideous injustice which in their name the Imperial ministers and their representatives in India have perpetrated. They will therefore remedy the two wrongs in accordance with the wishes of the people, and they will also offer a constitution exactly in accordance with the wishes of the people of India, as represented by their chosen leaders.

Supposing that the British Government wish to retire, because India is not a paying concern, what do you think will then be the position of India ?"

Mr. Gandhi answered : " At that stage surely it is easy to understand that India will then have evolved either outstanding spiritual height or the ability to offer violence against violence. She will have evolved an organising ability of a high order, and will therefore be in every way able to cope with any emergency that might arise."

" In other words," observed the *Times* representative, "you expect the moment of the British evacuation, if such a contingency arises, will coincide with the moment of India's preparedness and ability and conditions favourable for India to take over the Indian administration as a going concern and work it for the benefit and advancement of the Nation ? "

Mr. Gandhi answered the question with an emphatic affirmative. " My experience during the last months fills me with the hope," continued Mr. Gandhi, " that within the nine months that remain of the year in which I have expected Swaraj for India we shall redress the two wrongs and we shall see Swaraj established in accordance with the wishes of the people of India."

"Where will the present Government be at the end of the nine months?" asked the *Times* representative.

Mr. Gandhi, with a significant smile, said:—"The lion will then lie with the lamb."

Young India—29th December, 1920.

THE SWARAJ OF MY IDEAL

*[The following is the full text of the speech
delivered by Mahatma Gandhi at Calcutta
in December, 1920:—]*

Lord Ronaldshay who has done me the
honour of reading my booklet on Home Rule
has warned my countrymen against engaging
themselves in a struggle for a Swaraj such as
is described in that booklet. Now though I
do not want to withdraw a single word of it, I
would say to you on this occasion that I do
not ask India to follow out to-day the methods
prescribed in my booklet. If they could do
that they would have Home Rule not in a
year but in a day, and India by realising that
ideal wants to acquire an ascendency over the
rest of the world. But it must remain a day
dream more or less for the time being. What
I am doing to-day is that I am giving the
country a pardonable programme not the
abolition of law courts, posts, telegraphs and
of railways but for the attainment of Parliamentary Swaraj. I am telling you to do that
so long as we do not isolate ourselves from

this Government, we are co-operating with it through schools, law courts and councils through service, civil and military, and payment of taxes and foreign trade.

The moment this fact is realised and non-co-operation is effected, this Government must totter to pieces. If I knew that the masses were prepared for the whole programme at once, I would not delay in putting it at once to work. It is not possible, at the present moment, to prevent the masses from bursting out into wrath against those, who come to execute the law. It is not possible, that the military would lay down their arms without the slightest violence. If that were possible to-day, I would propose all the stages of non-co-operation to be worked simultaneously. But we have not secured that control over the masses; we have uselessly frittered away precious years of the nation's life in mastering a language which we need least for winning our liberty; we have frittered away all those years in learning liberty from Milton and Shakespeare, in deriving inspiration from the pages of Mill, whilst liberty could be learnt at our doors. We have thus succeeded in isolating ourselves from the masses; we have been

westernised. We have failed these 35 years
to utilise our education in order to permeate
the masses.   We have sat upon the pedestal
and from there delivered harangues to them
in a language they do not understand and we
see to-day that we are unable to conduct large
gatherings in a disciplined manner. And
discipline is the essence of success. Here is
therefore one reason why I have introduced
the word 'progressive' in the non-co-operation
Resolution. Without any impertinence I may
say that I understand the mass mind better
than any one amongst the educated Indians.
I contend that the masses are not ready
for suspension of payment of taxes.   They
have not yet learnt sufficient self-control.
If I was sure of non-violence on their part I
would ask them to suspend payment to-day
and not waste a single moment of the nation's
time.   With me the liberty of India has become a passion. Liberty of Islam is as dear to
me.   I would not therefore delay a moment if
I found that the whole of the programme
could be enforced at once.

It grieves me to miss the faces of dear and
revered leaders in this assembly. We miss
here the trumpet voice of Surendranath

Banerji, who has rendered inestimable service to the country. And though we stand as poles asunder to-day, though we may have sharp differences with him, we must express them with becoming restraint. I urge non-violence in language and in deed. If non-violence is essential in our dealings with the Government, it is more essential in our dealings with our leaders. And it grieves me deeply to hear of recent instances of violence reported to have been used in East Bengal against our own people. I was pained to hear that the ears of a man who had voted at the recent elections had been cut, and nights oil had been thrown into the bed of a man who had stood as a candidate. Non-co-operation is never going to succeed in this way. It will not succeed unless we create an atmosphere of perfect freedom, unless we prize our opponent's liberty as much as our own. The liberty of faith, conscience, thought and action which we claim for ourselves must be conceded equally to others. Non-co-operation is a process of purification and we must continually try to touch the hearts of those who differ from us, their minds, and their emotions, but never their bodies. Discipline and restraint are the cardinal principles of our conduct and

I warn you against any sort of tyranical
social ostracism.   I was deeply grieved therefore to hear of the insult offered to a dead body
in Delhi and feel that if it was the action of
non-co-operators they have disgraced themselves and their creed.   I repeat we cannot
deliver our land through violence.

It was not a joke when I said on the congress platform that Swaraj could be established
in one year if there was sufficient response from
the nation.   Three months of his year are
gone.   If we are true to our salt, true to our
nation, true to the songs we sing, if we are
true to the Bhagwad-Gita and the Koran, we
would finish the programme in the remaining
nine months and deliver Islam, the Punjab
and India.

I have proposed a limited programme
workable within one year, having special regard
to the educated classes. We seem to be labouring under the illusion that we cannot possibly
live without councils, law courts and schools
provided by the Government. The moment
we are disillusioned we have Swaraj. It is
demoralising both for Government and the go-
verned that a hundred thousand pilgrims should
dictate   terms to a nation   composed of

three hundred millions. And how is it they can thus dictate terms. It is because we have been divided and they have ruled. I have never forgotten Humes' frank confession that the British Government was sustained by the policy of "Divide and Rule." Therefore it is that I have laid stress upon Hindu Moslem Unity as one of the most important essentials for the success of Non-co-operation. But it should be no lip unity, nor bania unity, it should be a unity broadbased on a recognition of the heart. If we want to save Hinduism I say for God's sake, do not seek to bargain with the Musalman. I have been going about with Maulana Shaukat Ali all these months, but I have not so much as whispered anything about protection of the cow. My alliance with the Ali Brothers is one of honour. I feel that I am on my honour, the whole of Hinduism is on its honour, and if it will not be found wanting, it will do its duty towards the Musalmans of India. Any bargaining would be degrading to us. Light brings light not darkness, and nobility done with a noble purpose will be twice rewarded. It will be God alone who can protect cow. Ask me not to-day, ' what about the cow,' ask me after Islam is vindicated through India.   Ask the Rajas what they do to entertain their English guests.   Do they not provide beef and champaigne for their guests? Persuade them first to stop cow killing and then think of bargaining with Musalmans. And how are we Hindus behaving ourselves towards the cow and her progeny? Do we treat her as our religion requires us? Not till we have set our own house in order and saved the cow from the Englishmen, have we the right to plead on her behalf with the Musalmans. And the best way of saving the cow from them is to give them unconditional help in their hour of trouble.

Similarly what do we owe the Punjab? The whole of India was made to crawl on her belly in as much as a single Punjabi was made to crawl in that dirty lane in Amritsar; the whole womanhood of India was unveiled in as much as the innocent women of Manianwalla were unveiled by an insolent officer ; and Indian childhood was dishonoured in that, that school-children of tender age were made to walk four times a day to stated places within the Martial area in the Punjab and to salute the Union Jack, through the effect of which order two children, seven years old, died of sun

3

stroke having been made to wait in the noon-
day sun. In my opinion it is a sin to attend
the schools and colleges conducted under the
ægis of this Government so long as it has not
purged itself of these crimes by proper
repentance. We may not with any sense of
self-respect plead before the courts of the
Government when we remember that it was
through the Punjab Courts that innocent men
were sentenced to be imprisoned and hanged.
We become participators in the crime of the
Government by voluntarily helping it or being
helped by it.

The women of India have intuitively
understood the spiritual nature of the
struggle. Thousands have attended to
listen to the message of non-violent non-
co-operation and have given me their
precious ornaments for the purpose of
advancing the cause of Swaraj. Is it any
wonder if I believe the possibility of gaining
Swaraj within a year after all these wonderful
demonstrations? I would be guilty of want of
faith in God if I underrated the significance
of the response from the women of India. I
hope that the students will do their duty. The
country certainly expects the lawyers who

have hitherto led public agitation to recognise
the new awakening.

I have used strong language but I have
done so with the greatest deliberation. I am
not actuated by any feeling of revenge. I do
not consider Englishmen as my enemy. I
recognise the worth of many. I enjoy the
privilege of having many English friends, but
I am a determined enemy of the English rule
as is conducted at present and if the power—
tapasya—of one man could destroy it, I would
certainly destroy it, if it could not be mended.
An Empire that stands for injustice and
breach of faith does not deserve to stand if its
custodians will not repent and Non-co-operation has been devised in order to enable the
nation to compel justice.

I hope that Bengal will take her proper
place in this movement of self-purification.
Bengal began Swadeshi and national education
when the rest of India was sleeping. I hope
that Bengal will come to the front in this
movement for gaining Swaraj and gaining
justice for the Khilafat and the Punjab
through purification and self-sacrifice.

THE SECRET OF SWARAJ

The Congress resolution has rightly emphasised the importance of Swadeshi and the amount of greater sacrifice by merchants.

India cannot be free so long as India voluntarily encourages or tolerates the economic drain which has been going on for the past century and a half. Boycott of foreign goods means no more and no less than boycott of foreign cloth. Foreign cloth constitutes the largest drain voluntarily permitted by us. It means sixty crores of rupees annually paid by us for piecegoods. If India could make a successful effort to stop that drain, she can gain Swaraj by that one act.

India was enslaved for satisfying the greed of the foreign cloth manufacturer. When the East India Company came in, we were able to manufacture all the cloth we needed, and more for export. By processes that need not be described here, India has become practically wholly dependent upon foreign manufacture for her clothing.

But we ought not to be dependent. India has the ability to manufacture all her cloth if her children will work for it. Fortunately India has yet enough weavers to supplement the out-turn of her mills. The mills do not and cannot immediately manufacture all the cloth we want. The reader may not know that, even at the present moment, the weavers weave more cloth than the mills. But the latter weave five crore yards of fine foreign counts, equal to forty crore yards of coarser counts. The way to carry out a successful boycott of foreign cloth is to increase the output of yarn. And this can only be done by hand-spinning.

To bring about such a boycott, it is necessary for our merchants to stop all foreign importation, and to sell out, even at a loss, all foreign cloth already stocked in India, preferably to foreign buyers. They must cease to speculate in cotton, and keep all the cotton required for home use. They must stop purchasing all foreign cotton.

The mill-owners should work their mills not for their profits but as a national trust and therefore cease to spin finer counts, and weave only for the home market.

The householder has to revise his or her ideas of fashion and, at least for the time being, suspend the use of fine garments which are not always worn to cover the body. He should train himself to see art and beauty in the spotlessly white *khaddar* and to appreciate its soft unevenness. The householder must learn to use cloth as a miser uses his horde.

And even when the householders have revised their tastes about dress, somebody will have to spin yarn for the weavers. This can only be done by every one spinning during spare hours either for love or money.

We are engaged in a spiritual war. We are now living in abnormal times. Normal activities are always suspended in abnormal times. And if we are out to gain *Swaraj* in a year's time, it means that we must concentrate upon our goal to the exclusion of every thing else. I therefore venture to suggest to the students all over India to suspend their normal studies for one year and devote their time to the manufacture of yarn by hand-spinning. It will be their greatest act of service to the motherland, and their most natural contribution to the attainment of *Swaraj*. During the late war our rulers attempted to turn every

factory into an arsenal for turning out bullets
of lead. During this war of ours, I suggest
every national school and college being turned
into a factory for preparing cones of yarns for
the nation. The students will lose nothing by
the occupation : they will gain a kingdom here
and hereafter. There is a famine of cloth in
India. To assist in removing this dearth is
surely an act of merit. If it is sinful to use
foreign yarn, it is a virtue to manufacture
more Swadeshi yarn in order to enable us to
cope with the want that would be created by
the disuse of foreign yarn.

The obvious question asked would be, if it
is so necessary to manufacture yarn, why not
pay every poor person to do so ? The answer
is that hand-spinning is not, and never was, a
calling like weaving, carpentry, etc. Under
the pre-British economy of India, spinning
was an honourable and leisurely occupation
for the women of India. It is difficult to
revive the art among the women in the time
at our disposal. But it is incredibly simple
and easy for the school-goers to respond to the
nation's call. Let not one decry the work as
being derogatory to the dignity of men or
students. It was an art confined to the women

of India because the latter had more leisure. And being graceful, musical, and as it did not involve any great exertion, it had become the monopoly of women. But it is certainly as graceful for either sex as is music for instance. In hand-spinning is hidden the protection of women's virtue, the insurance against famine and the cheapening of prices. In it is hidden the secret of *Swaraj*. The revival of hand-spinning is the least penance we must do for the sin of our forefathers in having succumbed to the satanic influences of the foreign manufacturer.

The school-goers will restore hand-spinning to its respectable status. They will hasten the process of making *khaddar* fashionable. For no mother or father worth the name will refuse to wear cloth made out of yarn spun by their children. And the scholars, practical recognition of art will compel the attention of the weavers of India. If we are to wean the Punjabi from the calling not of a soldier but of the murderer of innocent and free people of other lands, we must give back to him the occupation of weaving. The race of the peaceful Julahis of the Punjab is all but extinct. It is for the scholars of the Punjab to make it possible for the Punjabi weaver to return to his innocent calling.

I hope to show in a future issue how easy it is to introduce this change in the schools and how quickly, on these terms, we can nationalise our schools and colleges. Everywhere the students have asked me what new things I would introduce into our nationalised schools. I have invariably told them I would certainly introduce spinning. I feel, so much more clearly than ever before that during the transition period, we must devote exclusive attention to spinning and certain other things of immediate national use, so as to make up for past neglect. And the students will be better able and equipped to enter upon the new course of studies.

Do I want to put back the hand of the clock of progress? Do I want to replace the mills by hand-spinning and hand-weaving? Do I want to replace the railway by the country cart? Do I want to destroy machinery altogether? These questions have been asked by some journalists and public men. My answer is: I would not weep over the disappearance of machinery or consider it a calamity. But I have no design upon machinery as such. What I want to do at the present moment is to supplement the production of yarn and cloth through our mill, save the millions we send out of India, and distribute them in our cottages. This I cannot do unless and until the nation is prepared to devote its leisure hours to hand-spinning. To that end we must adopt the methods I have ventured to suggest for popularising spinning as a duty rather than as a means of livelihood.

Young India—January 19, 1921.

TO YOUNG BENGAL

Dear Young Friends :—

I have just read an account of your response to the nation's call. It does credit to you and to Bengal. I had expected no less. I certainly expect still more. Bengal has great intelligence. It has a greater heart, it has more than its share of the spiritual heritage for which our country is specially noted. You have more imagination, more faith and more emotion than the rest of India. You have falsified the calumny of cowardice on more occasions than one. There is, therefore, no reason why Bengal should not lead now as it has done before now.

You have taken the step you will not recede. You had ample time to think. You have paused, you have considered. You held the Congress that delivered to the nation the message of Non-co-operation, *i.e.*, of self-purification, self-sacrifice, courage and hope. The Nagpur Congress ratified, clarified and amplified the first declaration. It was delivered in the midst of strife, doubt and disunion. I*t* was re-delivered in the midst of joy acclamation, and practically perfect unanimity. It was open to you to refuse, or to hesitate to respond. You have chosen the better, though, from a wordly wise standpoint, less cautious way. You dare not go back without hurting yourselves and the cause.

But for the evil spell that the existing system of government and, most of all, this western education has cast upon us, the question will not be considered as open to argument. Can the brave Arabs retain their independence and yet be schooled under the ægis of those who would hold them under bondage? They will laugh at a person who dared to ask them to go to schools that may be established by their invaders. Is the case different, or if it is different, is it not stronger in our case when we are called upon to give up schools conducted under the ægis of a government which, rightly or wrongly, we seek to bend to our will or destroy?

We cannot get *Swaraj* if not one class in the country is prepared to work and sacrifice for it. The Government will yield not to the logic of words. It knows no logic but that of brave and true deeds.

Bravery of the sword they know· And they have made themselves proof against its use by us. Many of them will welcome violence on our part· They are unconquerable in the art of meeting and suppressing violence· We propose, therefore, to sterilize their power of inflicting violence by our non·violence. Violence dies when it ceases to evoke response from its object. Non-violence is the corner-stone of the edifice of Non-co-operation. You will, therefore, not be hasty or overzealous in your dealings with those who may not see eye to eye with you. Intolerance is a species of violence and therefore against our creed. Non-violent Non-co-operation is an object lesson in democracy. The moment we are able to ensure non-violence, even under circumstances the most provoking, that moment we have achieved our end, because that is the moment when we can offer complete Non-co-operation·

I ask you not to be frightened at the pro-position just stated. People do not move in arithmetical progression, not even in geometri-cal progression. They have been known to perish in a day: they have been known to rise in a day. Is it such a difficult thing for India to realise that thirty crores of human

beings have but to feel their strength and
they can be free without having to use it ?
As we had not regained national Conscious-
ness, the rulers have hitherto played us
against one another. We have to refuse to do
so, and we are masters, not they.

Non-co-operation deals first with those
sensitive classes upon whom the government
has acted so successfully and who have been
lured into the trap consciously or unconsciously
as the school-going youths have been.

When we come to think about it, the
sacrifice required is infinitesimal for individuals,
because the whole is distributed among so
many of us. For what is your sacrifice ? To
suspend your literary studies for one year or
till Swaraj is established. If I could 'infect'
the whole of the student world with my faith,
I know that suspension of studies need not
extend even to a year.

And in the place of your suspended studies
I would urge you to study the methods of
bringing about Swaraj as quietly as possible
even within the year of grace. I present you
with the SPINNING WHEEL and suggest
to you that on it depends India's economic
salvation.

But you are at liberty to reject it if you wish and go to the College that has been promised to you by Mr. Das. Most of your fellow-students in the National College at Gujarat have undertaken to give at least four hours to spinning everyday. It is no sacrifice to learn a beautiful art and to be able to clothe the naked at the same time.

You have done your duty by withdrawing from Government colleges, I have only showed you the easiest and the most profitable way of devoting the time at your disposal.

May God give you strength and courage to sustain you in your determination.

Your well-wisher,
M. K. Gandhi.
Young India—19th January, 1921.

WHAT STUDENTS CAN DO

*[A monster public meeting was held at Mirza-
pur Square on 21st January, 1921, when
Mahatma Gandhi addressed the students
and said:—]*

Mr. Chairman and friends,—We are in
the throes of a new birth and we are experienc-
ing all the difficulties, all the pangs, all the
difficulties and all the pains that attend a new
birth. Let me congratulate the students of
Bengal on the very magnificent response you
have returned to the call of the country. I
knew that the students of Calcutta were wait-
ing for my friend Mr. C. R. Das to give them
the lead.

I congratulate him upon his having given
you the lead and I congratulate you the
students of Bengal, upon having followed that
lead. But you know as well as I do that the task
for him and for you has only just commenced.
It is not enough for him, it is not enough for
India that you have emptied the colleges. It
is absolutely necessary that you must not
return to the colleges and the schools that you

have abandoned and it is necessary for him to
find out for you the work that you should do,
during this period of probation, during this
period of purification.

It has now become necessary for Mr. C. R.
Das and for you to put your heads together and
devise means whereby you may complete the
work that you have begun. Any way you the
students who have withdrawn from the Government and Government aided schools have
completed your work. But in order that that
work may be sustained that work may be
continued and in order that your services may
be harnessed for the attainment of Swaraj, it
is necessary to find out the ways and means.
And it grieves me—I cannot describe to you
how grieved I am to find that whilst the
student world has responded so nobly, the professors and educationists and the trustees of
the great educational institutions of Bengal are
not responding in a manner in which they
might have. And in drawing your attention
and their attention to this fact, I do not wish
to be understood as casting any reflection upon
them, or their love for their country. I know,
I am convinced, that they believe that you have
erred. I know that they believe that Mr. Das

4

has erred in asking you not to seek shelter
behind your conscience but to respond to the
call of the nation. They believe that I am
grievously in error in having presented Non-
Co-operation to the country, and they sincerely
believe that I am still more grievously in
error in having advised the students to boycott
Government educational institutions. But
in spite of all the experience that I have gone
through, in spite of all that I have heard
and read and in spite of all the reverence
that I claim, I am capable of tendering to
our elders, and our leaders, I am here
to confess before you that I am more than ever
convinced of the correctness of the step that I
have suggested to the country. I am more
than ever convinced that if we desire to
establish Swaraj of our choice, I am more
than ever convinced that if we want to retrieve
the lost honour of India—if we want to
retrieve the honour of Islam which is trem-
bling in the balance it is absolutely necessary
for us to tell this Government that it shall not
receive any help from us, nor shall we receive
any help from a Government which has for-
feited all confidence. I know those of you who
are sceptics will tell me or tell yourselves th at

you have heard this kind of talk many a time
from platforms of this nature and it is true.
But Max Muller has told us—he has para-
phrased a Sanskrit proverb that a truth always
bears repetition until it has gone home and I
propose to reiterate this truth in the ears of
my countrymen—to reiterate this truth before
our elders till it goes home and till they
respond to it.   I am here to repeat what I
have said from so many platforms that India
will not regain her lost honour—her lost
freedom until India has responded to the call
of Non-co-operation (cheers)—it is not
possible—it is not possible for India, consti-
tuted as we are, to give battle to this great
Government on any other terms.   Non-co-
operation is bred in the very marrow of every
Indian, and if you want to know why the
crores and millions of the masses have
responded to the call of Non-co-operation as
they have never responded to any other call,
it is not because I gave voice to that call. But
it is because it is born, it is bred in them—it
is the part of every religion—it is the part of
Hinduism—it is part of Islam and it is for that
reason that fallen though we are, helpless
though we feel ourselves to be, Non-co-opera-

tion has awakened us from this long sleep. Non-co-operation has given us faith, has given us courage, has given us hope, has given us strength. And if our educated leaders have not yet responded to the call of Non-co-operation let me say with all the humility that I can command that they are sceptics, they have not the religious fire of the people and the masses. They are saturated in modern civilisation, or as we call it Western civilisation. I have used the term Western civilisation as synonymous with modern civilisation. But I want you and myself this evening to distinguish between Western civilisation and modern civilisation. I want you to understand that I am not a hater of the West. I am thankful to the West for many a thing I have learnt from Western literature. But I am here to confess to you—I am thankful to modern civilisation for teaching me that if I want India to rise to its highest height I must tell my countrymen frankly that after years and years of experience of modern civilisation, I have learnt one lesson from it and that is that we must shun it at all costs. What is that modern civilisation—it is the worship of the brute in us—it is the worship of the material, it is unadulterated materialism and modern civilisation is nothing if it does not think at every step the triumph of materialised civilisation. And if I did not know my country, if I did not know the mass mind, I would also have erred and I would also have been misled even as I contend that educated India has been misled. You, my countrymen, know that I have lived for 20 years in the midst of modern activity—I have lived in a country which has copied everything that is modern. I have lived in a country which is pulsating with new life. South Africa is a country which contains some of the bravest of men on the face of the earth, and I have seen modern civilisation worked by that nation at its best, and I am here to tell you the young men of Bengal and I am here to tell my educated leaders that my experience of modern civilisation worked at its best told me in emphatic terms in the year 1908. " God save India from that modern curse". (hear, hear). That was a lesson that I have learnt in South Africa though it is the lesson that I have followed up since 1908 and that is the lesson which slowly but surely I have been preaching in season and out of season

during my five years' stay in India and it was
my faith in our ancient civilisation—it was my
faith in our simplicity, it is my faith in inborn
religious instincts of every Indian be he a
Hindu or be he a Mahomedan, Christian, Parsi
or a Jew—it is that faith in me which has
sustained me throughout all the dark days, of
scoffing and scepticism and of opposition. I
know that opposition stares you and stares me
in the face even to-day. We have just
broken the ground but it is true that if
we are going to win this great battle that
you the people of Calcutta commenced in
September of last year—if we are going
to win this great battle we shall have to
continue as we have begun in full faith. I am
not ashamed to repeat before you who seem to
be nurtured on modern traditions—who seem
to be filled with the writings of modern writers,
I am not ashamed to repeat before you that this
is a religious battle. I am not ashamed to repeat
before you that this is an attempt to rovolu-
tionise the political outlook—that this is an
attempt to spiritualise our politics. And the
more we have of it, I assure you the greater
progress we shall make towards our goal. And
it is because I believe that the mass mind of

India is to-day ready and it is because I believe that the mass mind of India is tired of this British rule in its present form that I have made bold to say that Swaraj is easily attainable within one year (cries hear, hear.)

Four months of this one year have already gone by and my faith has never burnt as brightly as it burns to-night, as I am talking to the young men of Bengal (hear, hear). You have given me greater hope, you have given me greater courage, you have given me greater strength. May God grant that Shaukat Ali and Muhammad Ali and I will live to erect this flag of Swaraj inside this year? (hear, hear). But if it is the will of God that my ashes should be placed in the Ganges water before the eight months of the year is out, I shall die with the conviction that you will see to it that Swaraj is secured before the year is out.

This is not difficult as you imagine. The difficulty lies with our conviction. The difficulty lies in our believing that we want to have lessons in Swaraj in the Council hall. The difficulty lies in our believing that we cannot get Swaraj until we have passed through a sixteen years' course of education, and if we believe in all these things I shall be free to confess that we should require a century to get Swaraj. But it is because I believe that we need not these things, but we require strength, we require courage, we require faith, and it is because I believe that the masses have got all these things to-day that I believe that Swaraj is attainable within this year.

And what does the appeal of the Congress mean? The Congress appeal means that you and I that the whole of educated India, the whole of the mercantile community of India— a mere drop in the ocean of millions of people of India, the artisans and the agriculturists— have a test placed before them. And believe me that the Congress will isolate India and wrest Swaraj from insolent hands and establish the flag of Freedom, if possible with your assistance, even without your assistance if need be. The whole of India is not concentrated in the educated India of to-day. India can sustain its hope even if the whole of educated India were to remain without hope and faith and courage and strength. And it is that faith which sustains me. But I am hoping that if the student World and I am hoping if the students of Bengal remain true to their conviction, remain true to their vow, I am hoping that the professors and the trustees and the educationists of Bengal and India will respond to the call and their winter of discontent will be turned by you into the summer of hope. But I ask you, the young men of Bengal, to abide by the decision that you have come to—no matter what happens. I know that Mr. C. R. Das is going to remain true to his promise (hear, hear). He has already received a promise of Rs. 10,000 to be given to him now and ten thousand annual contribution from a great Bengali. He has received certain promises from the Marwaris—the domiciled Marwaris of Calcutta—and he is going to receive many more promises, so far as the finance is concerned, but finance is the least part of the difficulty (hear, hear). He has to find out a habitation for having the college located. He has to find out better professors. And I ask you those students who have non-co-operated not to set before yourselves the old standard even as this Swaraj of our dream is not to be a base copy of what we have to-day. So will you please see that what you get in the shape of a new college is not to be a base copy of what you have to-day. You will not look to

brick and mortar. You will not look to
benches and chairs for inspiration. But you
will look to character. You will look to sterling character in your professors and in your
teachers for inspiration. You will look to your
own strength and to your own determination to
give you the necessary impetus and necessary
inspiration. And I promise to you that you
will then not be disappointed, but if you believe
that Mr. Das is going to present you with
noble buildings, if you believe that he is going
to give every ease and luxury to which you
have hitherto been used, you will certainly be
disappointed. But I have come this evening
to present before you a newer gospel, a better
gospel. If you are determined to attain
Swaraj inside of twelve months, if you are
determined to help to attain Swaraj within
one year then I ask you to make his way
clearer, easier, ask you to make the way of
those who have dedicated their lives to the
attainment of Swaraj easier and clearer by
accepting the advice that I am about to tender
to you.

If you believe that Swaraj can be attained
by continuing your colleges and schools
precisely in the same manner as the institutions

that you have left are being conducted you are sadly mistaken. No country in the world has gained its liberty—has attained a new birth without difficulties, without pain, without sacrifice. And what is sacrifice ? The right meaning of sacrifice I learnt in my youth was that it meant, making sacred, making holy. Non-co-operation is a process of purification and if a suspension of our ordinary routine is necessary for the purpose of that purification that has to be done. I know, if I know Bengal at all that you will not shirk it and you will respond. Our education has been the most deficient in two things. Those who formed our education code neglected the training of the body and the Soul. You are receiving the education of the soul but the very fact of Non-co-operation for Non-co-operation is nothing less and nothing more than withdrawing from participation in the evil that this Government is doing and continuing to do. And if we are withdrawing from evil conscientiously, deliberately, it means that we are walking with our face towards God. That completes or begins the soul training. But seeing that our bodily education has been neglected and seeing that

India has become enslaved because India forgot the spinning wheel and because India sold herself for a mess of pottage, I am not afraid to place before the youngmen of Bengal, the Spinning Wheel for adoption. And let a training in spinning and production of as much yarn as you can ever do constitute your main purpose and your main training during this year of probation. Let your ordinary education commence after Swaraj is established. But let every youngman and every girl of Bengal consider it to be their sacred duty to devote all their time and energy to spinning. I have drawn attention to the parallel that presents itself before us, from the War.

Those of you who know anything about what was going on in England will recall those days of the War when every boy and every girl had suspended their education—ordinary education, and they were put upon such national work as was necessary for the purpose of the War. They were put upon simple tailoring upon making badges and that was done even here. I recall many a home where even little children were put to work and the Government looked upon my activity with sympathy, with attention and approval when I presented to the youths of Khaira the opportunity of fighting on the battle field even though their parents might be against it. Times have changed and I am now twitted for asking youngmen who have got heads on their shoulders and who have a conscience in their hearts—I am twitted for asking these youngmen and girls and for having the audacity to tell them that they should rather obey the voice of their conscience than the voice or commands of even of their parents. But I say to the youngmen and young girls of Bengal that if your voice, the voice of your conscience tells you that during this year of probation you should devote your energy and attention to the attainment of Swaraj then you will believe me when I tell you that it is impossible to arrive at a complete boycott of foreign cloth or foreign goods until and unless we would employ every man, woman and child to spinning yarn. We have spun many a yarn during all these long 35 years on the Congress platform (laughter). Enough of it. Let us now spin the truest yarn that India wants and let me tell you that if you want to feed the hungry, to clothe the naked there is no other way out of

the difficulty but spinning for the whole of
India. And so I ask you youngmen of Bengal
to accept the privilege that I place at your feet,
And if we can bring a complete boycott of foreign cloth we sterilise the activity of the fifty-
five Members of the House of Commons
that Lancashire contributes to it, we sterilise
the activities of ambitious Japan who has her
eyes fixed and set upon India. And you will
not gain your economic freedom, as the Congress
has told you until India becomes self-contained
so far as her food and clothing are concerned.
We can do without all things but we cannot do
without food and clothing. And a vast country
like India 1900 miles long and 1500 miles
broad cannot possibly become self-contained
by any other means than the means of old.

So youngmen of Bengal if you will work in
order to gain Swaraj within one year you will
accept the advice of a man who has conducted
a series of experiments to whom this gospel
came in the year 1908 and who has not yet
been ousted from it by a hair's breadth. The
more I have studied the economics of India, the
more I have listened to the mill-owners of
India the more convinced I have become that
until we introduce the spinning wheel in every

home of India, the economic salvation and freedom of India is an impossibility. Go to any mill-owner you like he will tell you that it will require fifty years if India is to become self-contained so far as cloth supplies are concerned if she has to depend upon her mills alone. And let me supplement the information by telling you that to-day hundreds and thousands of weavers are weaving and are able to weave home-spun yarn because mills cannot supply them. So I ask the young friends of Bengal who have left their colleges to go forward in hope and courage and take up this neglected training of the hand for at least the time that we have not attained Swaraj and then think of anything else.

I have suggested another thing. You and I, every one of us has neglected the true education that we should have received in our national schools. It is impossible for the young men of Bengal for the young men of Gujrat—for the young men of the Deccan to go to the Central Provinces, to go to the United Provinces, to go to the Punjab and all those vast tracts of India which speak nothing but Hindustani, and therefore I ask you to learn Hindusthani also in your leisure hours—

the hours that you may be able to save after
spinning. And if you will learn these things
you can learn both spinning and Hindusthani
in two months. An intelligent, gentle lad—a
patriotic and hardworking lad, I promise you,
can learn both these in two months' time.
And then you are free to go out to your
villages—you are free to go to every part of
India but Madras, and be able to speak your
mind to the masses. Do not consider for one
moment that you can possibly make English
a common medium of expression between the
masses. Twenty-two crores of Indians know
Hindustani—they do not know any other
language. And if you want to steal into the
hearts of 22 crores of Indians, Hindusthani
is the only language open to you, if you will
do but these two things, during this year—
during these nine months, believe me you will
have by the time you have finished, acquired
courage and acquired strength which you do
not possess to-day. I know thousands of
students—blank despair stares them in the
face if they are told that they cannot get
Government employ. And if you are bent
upon destroying or mending this Government
how do you propose to get Government employ?

And if you do not want to fall back upon Government what is your English knowledge worth ? I do not wish to underrate the literary value of the English language. I have suggested to the youngmen of Gujarat that they should suspend their literary training in English for these nine or twelve months and devote their time and energy and their leisure to learning spinning and to learning Hindusthani and then place themselves at the disposal of India, and join the national service that is going to be formed.   You are not going to respond to the great constitution that the Congress has given unless we have got an army of workers penetrating the seven and a half lakhs of villages with which India is studded, and if we are going to set up a rival organisation in every village of India and if we are going to have a representative of the Congress in every village of India we cannot do so until and unless the youngmen of India respond to the call of the Motherland. The privilege to pay is yours. The call to-day has come to the youngmen of Bengal and the rest of India. And I hope, I have every confidence that all the youngmen and all the young girls of India will respond to this sacred call. And I promise that before the year is

5

out you will not have regretted the day that
you set your heart upon these two things, and
you will find at the end of the chapter that
what I am saying to you to-night has come
true and that you have vindicated the honour
of India—you have vindicated the honour of
Islam and you have vindicated the honour of
the whole nation and established Swaraj. May
God grant you the youngmen and the young
girls of Bengal the necessary courage, the
necessary hope, the necessary confidence to go
through the sacred period of purification and
sacrifice. May God help you.

   Mahatma Gandhi, resuming, said :—There
was one thing which I have purposely neglected. I had the thing in my mind, but as I
was obliged to take up so much of your time as
to the necessity of spinning and the necessity
of learning Hindusthani and as to what you
should do after having given up your colleges,
I purposely omitted reference to the difficulty
of the medical students. If they will but
exercise their splendid faculty and imagination
they will deduce from what I have said
generally to the student world that the remarks
that are applicable to the arts colleges and
other colleges are equally applicable to the

medical students, if possible even much more to the medical students than to the others. They want to heal the bleeding wounds of India—they want to heal the diseases from which India is suffering and I know no greater wound than has been inflicted upon the Punjab and I know no greater disease than the disease of helplessness, dependence and servility from which the whole of India is suffering, and if the medical students will be true to their future calling they will have no hesitation in responding to the call. And they will have no hesitation in undertaking the humanitarian work of clothing the naked and of ridding India of her shame, degradation and helplessness. They cannot do any nobler work. For an Indian, no matter how noble, how learned, how powerful and rich he may be, there can be no nobler work than the work of attaining Swaraj—than the work of ridding India of the great disease from which we have been suffering from years and years. And so I ask all the medical students and all the boys of the colleges and all the boys over sixteen years of the schools without a moment's hesitation first of all to leave their schools and colleges to finish that one peremptory duty that devolves upon them. But it will always be open to you either to reject or accept my advice. It will be open to you to establish new colleges, new schools, new medical colleges or anything you like. But if you will accept my advice, you will understand that you will not have finished your work as true and brave fellows unless you dedicate all the time at your disposal for the attainment of Swaraj and make the task easy all round.

If there is anything that I have left out in connection with the medical college or any other institution and if you want a solution about these things from my lips I shall be prepared to answer these questions, but I must confess to you that I am tired of answering questions, I am tired of making speeches—I am tired of making appeals. I would far rather wish that I became speechless and left you to your own resources and left you to your own conscience. Only to-day I have been answering a correspondent who has written to the Nabajeeban, asking—" If you say, if you call, conscience above all, why do you waste so much of your time in arguing with us. Why do you not leave us to ourselves?" In a way the rebuke was well administered. But I know that the fire that is burning within me, I should be untrue to you and to myself if I do not give it to you in the best manner that I can and so I have been travelling through the length and breadth of India in order to give you the gospel of hope and courage that is within me. But believe me, if I could possibly be left alone, you will find me spinning away for all I am worth and pouring over the pages of Hindusthani books. I know that I can speak Hindusthani but I know my limitations also. And I know what handicap I am labouring under for though I am not so well versed in Hindusthani literature as I am in English literature.

And so, my young friends, I would ask you to cast all your doubts, all your fear, all your scepticism into the Bay of Bengal and rise with a new hope that will not be denied. (Continued cheers and cries of 'Bande Mataram.')

WHAT MERCHANTS CAN DO

[A meeting of the merchants of Burrabazar was held at Calcutta on January 30, 1921, when Mahatma Gandhi delivered the following address to them on their duties at the present moment :—]

Brothers, you all know that I speak seated on a chair and I feel ashamed on that account. I hope that I may not ever sit on a chair but I am helpless. As I want to win Swaraj in nine months, so I do not want these. My brothers gave me much trouble when I came through streets. I see that they love me much, but I want to dissuade them from that if I can. Outside this hall so many have assembled that no business can go on. Because of that, I lost half an hour. The reason is that the organisation has not been a good one. That ought not to be so. When it is known that many men will gather, provision will have to be made for that also. Work must not suffer and passages ought not to be blocked and tramcars ought not to be stopped. Our people's time ought not to be

wasted. There are a thousand people inside
and another thousand outside. Two thousand
hours of people's time have here been wasted.
I want that Hindi and Urdu papers should
also publish that touching the feet is bad, and
my request is that people should not do it.
I am greatly disturbed with noise, I am far
from well and cannot tolerate sound. "Bande
Mataram," "Mahatma Gandhi ki Jai"—these
shouts are of no avail unless they voice forth
our true feeling. What I mean to say is that
men do not translate into action what they
utter. I also have become a Kshatriya giving
up my Bania Dharma. Had I not been a
Kshatriya I would have demonstrated my
feelings by weeping. Certainly I am not thirst-
ing after touching of my feet by you. When I
shall want it I will plainly let you know my
feelings and that will be when my object will
be attained. I consider myself compromised
in dignity, otherwise Swaraj will be attained
in nine months. Let all of you combine and
lend a helping hand. There is no necessity
for shouting "Bande Mataram," "Hindu
Mussalman-ki-Jai," "Alla-ho-Akbar." What I
propose to do I shall accomplish certainly. I
must attain Swaraj. If thirty crores of people

say that they are not with me, yet I shall do
my work and win Swaraj but I do not like
shouting. In the matter of shouts and noise
I am like a weak lamb. Also prostration at the
feet is not good. Bow to all with your hands
folded. No one is worthy of being touched at
the feet, especially in this Kali yuga. The
times are changed. If you wish to accomplish
the work of 30 crores of men, then come out
with your money. Try to have money and
ask me to give account for the same. Appoint
some one treasurer. If you know that you
yourselves cannot attain Swaraj, then help
one with money.

If you do not help with money, Swaraj
will be difficult, but not impossible to attain.
If the students of India do not help me, it does
not matter. If the pleaders do not help it does
not matter.

If monied men do not help with money,
that also does not matter. The attainment of
Swaraj depends on the workers and the
agriculturists. I belong to the same profession
as yourselves by birth and was a merchant myself by profession. I was a lawyer and earned
money thereby. I am a student also and I think
that I am a good student too. If you have

power, if you have strength in you, if you want
to govern India, then make sacrifices. Sacrifice
yourselves, your children and your parents,
everything in your life. Swaraj depends upon
the agriculturists. If they do not help, then
Swaraj cannot be attained. If they co-operate
with the Government, then all your virtues
will not help you in winning Swaraj. If 25
crores of people turn out to be undutiful,
Swaraj cannot be attained. Now our Marwari
brothers, the President has just said that rich
have not turned up for to-day's meeting. This
pains me much. But there is a reason for it.
They have been brought up under this Government and they have made their piles under its
protection. They have earned their money with
their co-operation. So they are afraid of them.
The English people make money through
the co-operation of Indians. This truth is
not realised by my Marwari brothers. I do
not ask you to give up trade, but I ask
you to carry on honest business, and not
indulge in untruth. You may say that
if you do not resort to untruth, then you will
become fakirs. I think it is better to be fakirs,
and in that case I do not want any money from
you. You should give up trade of foreign goods

and as to your trade of foreign cloths that
should certainly be shunned. Those who fear
God, they cannot but do the work of God.
God has given you riches and that riches help
you to decorate your bodies. With that riches
you wear Malmal Pagrees. I ask you to be
fearless and wear Khaddar Pagrees, and give
up all connection with mills even in the matter
of agencies. I asked my son to give up this
business as it is not Swadeshi work and deal
in Khaddar. He answered—"Father Khaddar
business does not go on. Much of it is lying in
stock." Khaddar, Garah Khadi—whatever you
call it, such beautiful stuff cannot be found.
My brothers and sisters, all use it and the
labourers who are my brothers prepare it. The
exploitations which the mill-owners are making
are very unjust. When the price of cotton is
Rs. 9 how is it that the price of the yarn is
Rs. 34 ? I know that there is very little profit
in Khaddar business. The cause of this is the
mill-owners who increase the price of the yarn.
We have to clothe the shoe-makers and the
sweepers. If there be any Vaishnab in the
meeting he will say that the remnants of his
dish and dirty worn out clothes will suffice.
But I remember them in the morning and

consider them to be equal to me. If you wear Khaddar after leaving mill cloths, then its price will go up.

If you go to Janakpuri, Orissa, you will see the condition of the poor very miserable. Chattu may be had 'for food, but not ghee. When I was travelling in third class—as you of course do not, then I used to see in Dharmashalas that one man took out a handful of Chattu from his baggage, a little of salt and a read pepper—and with these mixed with water, he had his meal. I have turned out a Kshatriya and not a drop of water came to my eyes. In this country of Annapurna, ghee is not available. In Champaran, people are dying of starvation. There is one remedy for all these, and that is the only remedy for all these and that is Charka, If all women and girls spin yarn, then they will be able to feed themselves as the prices of Khaddar will look up then. If Swaraj is attained, then malmal also will be manufactured. I myself am a good workman and I can work it, but I say that you have got to make thread from No. 6 to 20 and that will be used in making saris and pathis. No. 80 thread has been used in making your pagrees. It is foreign and it is irreligion. The Marwaris have given up their religion.

If you wish to save cows then save Khilafat. Millionaries speak of stopping cow killing but co-operate with the English. Oppressive Englishmen drink the blood of cows. Agency of English goods is irreligious. It is said against the Musalmans that they kill cows. But I say that what is slaughtered in Bandara in five years cannot be done in 2 years by 7 crores of Musalmans. I repeat to you some commonplace things. It is about Champaran ? I narrated the matter to a Marwari and he burst into tears, I did not shed any tears. I drew his attention to the condition of a bullock drawing a cart. You worship cows, and are you justified in killing bullock ? See the condition of dairy farms. The cows give milk, the buffaloes also give milk. Milk is drawn in such quantities from their udders that blood comes out. And we drink it. If you truly wish to save cows, then come to the help of Khilafat. The Musalmans are not ungrateful but you should not ask him to save cows first before you can help his Khilafat. Don't do so—this is no matter of bargain. Die for your brothers, adopt Fakir and claim you are a Hindu. As a Hindu you should not turn out to be cowards but be bold in your conduct.

Give up your foreign trade, not all immediately but of piece-goods only, clear your house of foreign cloth and ask your mothers and wives to throw them out and not to wear them again. This will not cause you any loss. Send all those to South Africa and sell them there. They will be in demand there as there are no spinning machines there. India rested on the Dharma of faithful wives. Mussalman women do much work on Charkas.

If you have goods lying-in-stock sell it or burn it and promise that you will never purchase it or wear it. Make the weaver understand that foreign yarns should not be used. Ask them to despatch the goods which they have in stock and not to use yarn above No. 20 and use cloths made with them. I want three things. The first thing is "save me." Do not worry Gandhi, do not give him trouble and cry "Gandhi ki Jai" and consider it as harm. The second thing is—Money is needed. Give as much as you can afford, and do as much as you can. To-day the dealers in deeds have given me Rs. 10,000 and promised to give more by raising fresh subscriptions. I want that whatever you give you should give with humility and generosity. As I pray to God so I pray to you. Kindle your religious sense and your patriotic feelings. The third thing is this—be pure, be patriotic, be devoted to the cause of Swaraj and Khilafat. Khilafat is Kamdhenu. Use pure Swadeshi things in your household. This alone will do you good; 60 crores of rupees go out of the country. Save them and win Swaraj in nine months. Brothers, you have listened to me with such love and attention I am very pleased with you. But I do not want blind, mad love for me. I want the conscious love of India. With such love for me, I shall be able to free India. Again I ask you to remember my words and pray to God that, He may give you and me power to win Swaraj and bless you. With these words I conclude my speech.

After his address, brisk collections of money went on and quite a large sum was collected on the spot.

THE DUTY OF
POST-GRADUATE & LAW STUDENTS

[A meeting of the Post-graduate and law students of Calcutta was held at the Star Theatre on 29th January, 1921, when Mr. Gandhi addressed them on the present movement and their duty.]

The only excuse I could offer for being so horribly late is, this pile containing money and jewellery which your Marwari sisters have given for your sake. I had the pleasure and privilege of addressing them just now and the response that they made—the so-called uncultured ladies of Marwar—was a magnificent response. I do not believe there is anything under Rs. 10,000 worth of jewellery and cash in that pile. I know you will be pleased to hear from me that more is to be expected from our sisters this very afternoon. Do you therefore wonder if you find me saying in season and out of season, that I do expect "Swaraj" within one year? If the response in money, in men and in every respect continues as it has begun, the most confirmed sceptic will be converted

to the view that I venture to hold, and I ask
all the Post-graduate students who have
gathered here, to listen to your leaders, to
respond to the resolution of the Congress,
nay more, to respond to the voice of your own
conscience. If you are satisfied that we cannot
live under this Government with any degree
of self-respect, if you are satisfied that
this Government has trodden under foot
some of our most sacred sentiments, that
it has disregarded some of the inestimable privileges which we hold, you will come
to the same conclusion that the Congress has
come to ; that association with that Government is a crime, is a sin, and if you endorse
that view, it is impossible for us to receive any
instructions at the hands of or under the influence of a Government so wicked as ours.
The Duke of Connaught came to Calcutta
yesterday, and you saw what the great citizens
of Calcutta had to say about his visit. They
carried out complete 'Hartal.' Do you suppose
that for a man like me who has always tender-
ed the heartiest and voluntary co-operation to
this Government for a period of nearly 30 years
—do you suppose that it was a matter of pleasure to me that I should associate myself and

heartily entirely with a complete boycott of his visit? It was not a pleasure to me. At the same time I feel it to be my duty not only not to associate myself with it, but to propagate the idea that to extend any welcome to any representative of the Sovereign would be a mistake, would be a crime, would be inconsistent with our self-respect and that is the view I hold even up to the present moment. The Duke of Connaught has come, not to wipe your and my tears. He has come not to wipe away the insult that has been hurled against Islam and the seven crores of Mohamedans of India. He has come not to heal the wounds of the Punjab but he has come to sustain the powers which has been so horribly abused. He has come to add prestige to an institution which we consider to be corrupt at its very source and therefore it became our duty to boycott that visit, and our duty not to receive any instructions under the influence of that Government. And I, therefore, suggest to you, post-graduate students of Calcutta, that you would far rather postpone your further literary progress and throw in your lot with the millions of your countrymen and gain 'Swaraj' inside of one year. If you feel that by con-

6

tinuing your post-graduate studies under the
influence of this Government you can advance
by one single minute the establishment of
'Swaraj' on this great soil, I have no word to
say. But if you are convinced as I am convinced that continuation of our studies under
the ægis of this Government can only retard
our progress towards the goal, you will not
take one single minute before retiring from
these studies. I want you to face this question boldly and fairly. You are not called upon
to withdraw because the system of education
is rotten, rotten though it undoubtedly is. You
are called upon to suspend your studies, to
withdraw from the institution because they
are under the ægis of the Government which
you and I want to destroy if we cannot mend it.
And if we approach the question with that
view you will not ask any further question as
to your future. Your future is safe and insur-
ed, immediately you come out of these
institutions in order to advance the cause of
'Swaraj.' Your future rests not on these institutions but on yourselves. That is the lesson
which the Congress resolution teaches you and
teaches me. Hitherto for a period of 35 years
all our resolutions have been addressed to the

Government. The Congress has altered its
course. The Congress has asked the nation to
become introspective. The Congress has turned this searchlight inward. The Congress
addresses its resolution now not to the Government but to the nation. Its prayer is addressed to you, the student world of Calcutta and
to me an old man passed the stage of youth.
The Congress addresses its resolution and its
prayers to the uncultured men of India—the
people living on the field of India, to the
artisans and to all those whom we consider to
be the illiterate masses of India. And the
question that rises before you this afternoon is
what are you, the post-graduate students,
going to do? What part are you going to play
in this great upheaval. Are you going to be
mere witnesses or are you going to be actors?
Are you going to throw yourselves in the thick
of the fight and claim the laurel of victory? I
hope that your decision will be sound, swift
and certain, and after having come upon that
decision I hope that there will be no shirking
back. And I ask the students who are gathered in this theatre to burn their book and not
to seek at the present moment a literary
career. I ask you to work as hewers of wood

and drawers of water for the sake of "Swaraj." I therefore ask every one of you, students, to take to spinning wheel and you will find the message of the spinning wheel to be true.

The message of the spinning wheel is that he who takes me, he who turns me, brings 'Swaraj' within a measurable distance. The message of spinning wheel is that every man, woman or child of India will turn me for one year or eight months, and I shall present in turn 'Swaraj'. And I ask you to take that message from that wheel which costs no more than Rs. 7 or Rs. 8. Mr. Das was telling me only the other day that there is a Bengali song about the spinning wheel and the song runs somewhat thus, that the spinning wheel gives you all. That the spinning wheel is the cow of plenty, and I assure you that if you ask those who have taken to the spinning wheel they will tell you, "Yes," the spinning wheel is the Kamdhenu for ourselves."

The women who surrounded me this afternoon asked me to give them a message. As I went round them asking for donations for your sake they asked me for a message and my unhesitating message was "Take the spinning wheel. Purify yourselves, sacrifice yourselves for the sake of the country," and that is my humble message to you also. Purify yourselves by withdrawing yourselves from slave-owning institutions and take up the spinning wheel, and if you will do that I promise you 'Swaraj' within one year."

APPEAL TO MARWARI LADIES

[On Friday, the 4th February, 1921, a largely attended meeting of the ladies of Bara Bazar was held in the Thakurbari of Gopeshwar Mullicke, situated in Sinduriapaty, when Mahatmaji spoke to the following effect:—]

My dear sisters,—My words fail to give an adequate expression to the joy I am exercising at your sight. Wherever I go I request my sisters to bless me so that I may be successful in my mission. You all should preserve peace and tranquility and should not make noise. The kingdom, we went to see established is a kingdom not inferior to one which was ruled by our God-incarnate Ramchandra, and for this, piety and purity of heart are indispensable. Some one told me that the men work over much, but the women do not. I admit that the men are persevering workers but I dare say that the women too are not inferior to them in this point. My advice is that every woman should learn to be brave, truthful and pure. There is no one in this world who can be an equal of a woman who possesses a pure and kind heart. This spinning wheel which is before you is as pure as anything. Every one, in order that he or she may attain purity of the head and heart, should use it. Each and every woman of Gujarat uses this spinning wheel and our sisters of the Punjab are vying with her on that point. They produce very nice home-woven coarse cloth and present the same in a large quantity. My Marwari sister have, so to say, forgotten the use of this spinning wheel. They should be as brave as their Punjabi sisters and should daily work at the spinning wheel continually for two or three hours and thereby produce home-spun sacred thread. By so doing, they will be able to supply their sisters with cloth. You should all renounce your foreign-made *saris* and betake the use of the sacred and pure home-woven coarse cloth. I am trying my level best to remove those of your sisters, who are engaged in stone-breaking, from their work and to give them their daily wages. I request you to supply me with the price of cotton for them. A woman who possesses a pure heart needs no ornaments to beautify her person. I am in need of gifts from you all, which will enable me to clothe many of your naked sisters.

[No sooner the word "gifts" fell from the lips of Mahatmaji than there arose a bustle among the ladies present who, one and all, stood up to make their desired gifts and the rest of Mahatmaji's speech was drowned in the hubbub that followed. The ladies, then encircled Mahatmaji, who stood up and began to accept the presents made by them. There was a shower of gold bracelets, bangles, anklets, ear-rings and silver ornaments of various kinds- One young Marwari lady presented Mahatmaji with Rs. 500 in cash, while another vied with her by presenting ornaments of about 100 tolas of silver and 25 tolas of gold. It is estimated that Mahatmaji received presents amounting to more than Rs. 5,000 which included both cash and ornaments.]

THE DUTY OF STUDENTS

[*The opening ceremony of the National College, Calcutta, under the auspices of the Board of Education, recently formed by Srijuts Chittranjandas, Jitendralal Banerjee and other Non-co-operation leaders, took place on Friday, the 4th February, 1921. A hymn from the Gita was sung by a number of boys at the commencement.*

In opening the College, Mr. Gandhi addressed the students and professors as follows: —]

Friends,—You have just now heard the beautiful prayer sung by the students over there, and I hope that all of you will ponder over the magnificent language of that prayer. If we will base all our acts in this institution on prayer, I have very little doubt that we shall come through with added glory to ourselves and to our country. I have had the privilege, during these few months, of opening several institutions in several parts of India. But I must confess to you that, in opening no other institution have I been so weighed down with anxiety and fear as I am in performing the opening ceremony in connection with this institution. As I have elsewhere remarked, all the eyes, all the attention of the student world are centred upon Calcutta. You have seen so many telegrams reproduced in the press, I have seen many more telegrams not reproduced in the press, congratulating the students on the magnificent response to the country's call. You may have also noticed that as a result of your response the students all over India are withdrawing themselves from Government institutions. Great, therefore, is your responsibility and the responsibility of the professors and teachers connected with this institution, of Mr. Das and myself also. For myself, I can only assure you that my prayers will attend all your efforts in making this institution a success. But I know that no prayer that I can offer, no prayer that our clearer hearts can offer, can be of the slightest service unless the student approach their task in humility and in their fear of God, with perseverance, with single-mindedness and with love and a devotion for the country in whose name and for whose sake they have abandoned Government institutions. It is not a light task for a student expecting certificates of high merit, expecting a great career in his own estimation. It is no light task for a student with all these expectations to surrender them in the hope that he is rendering a service to the country and therefore a service to himself. Personally I have not the slightest doubt about it. I hope you will never have to regret the day that you left Government institutions. But I know also that you must have to regret the day if you will not use your time usefully, if you have left under the impulse of moment as so many of our leaders who mean well of the country have already expressed their fears. Let me hope that you will falsify their fears.

You will at the end of the year so discharge yourselves that those who are to-day filled with doubts may come forward with an expression of opinion that their doubts were misplaced. Let me not conceal from you, the students of Calcutta, what certificate Indians in other parts of India give to you. Many of the students, and many grown up men also, who have talked to me about your movement have expressed a sense of nervous fear. You have been credited with a great deal of emotion, you have been credited with a great deal of

impulsiveness, but you have not been credited
with the same amount of perseverance and
industry.

You are embarking upon a new career.
You are turning over a new leaf. You are
shouldering a great responsibility. You are
counting yourselves among the makers of
India of the future. And if you realise this
responsibility, I have no doubt, you will dispel
all these fears which have been expressed in
other parts of India. Those who know Bengal
well are in a position also to testify that
Bengalis on many an occasion have not been
found wanting; and for my part I shall
certainly decline to believe that those students
who have responded and who will join this
institution will be found wanting. I shall
hope also that the professors and the teachers
will prove true to their trust. What I said in
all humility to the professors and teachers at
the time of performing the opening ceremony
of the Gujarat National College, I am tempted
to repeat here; that the success and failure of
this institution will very largely depend upon
the honest exertion that the professors and
teachers may put forth. At this critical moment in the history of our dear country every

one of us, who intends to mould the young
mind of the country, has a serious responsibility, and if the professors and the teachers are
found asleep, if they are overtaken with doubt,
if they are overtaken with fear as to the future,
God help the students who come under their
charge. And I shall pray to the Almighty
that he may bless the professors and teachers
with wisdom, with courage, with faith and
with hope.

I have in one of my speeches told the
students that whilst they might go on with
the course that they have mapped out
for themselves they must not interfere with
others. You have perhaps read the paragraph that appeared in the newspaper to-
day with reference to Barisal. I do not
know whether it is an exaggerated account
of what had happened there. I do not care
whether it is an exaggeration and whether
it is an under statement, but it furnishes a
lesson for you and for me that we must on no
account resort to violence, that we must on no
account exert undue pressure. And as I said
at one of the meetings day before yesterday, I
hope that the students will not sit *dhurna*—
they will not exercise any pressure whatsoever

upon those students who would not come out
of the schools and colleges. It is sufficient faith
in that those who feel it is sinful to belong to
these institutions ought to come out of them.
If we have sufficient faith in ourselves we shall
remain steadfast although not a single other
student responds to the call. It does betray
want of faith in our own mission when you
become impatient. And if we are impatient
we begin to compel others to do what we have
done. I hope no one of the student who will
belong to this institution will be filled with
any such doubts as to the correctness of his
conduct.

I hope also that when I renew your acquaint-
ance a month hence, as I hope I shall be
able to do, you will not call upon me to address
you any longer in English, but that you will
have mastered sufficient Hindusthani to
be able to understand whatever message I
might have to give to you in our national
common language· I assure you when
you approach your study of Hindusthani
some of you will find it simple and easy. To
some of you the words will seem perfectly
natural, because the vocabulary is common to
Bengali, Hindi and most of the Indian

languages, barring the Dravidian stock. You will find also it will feed your intellect and it will satisfy all the intellectual requirements of intellectual Bengal. And if you want to go in for literature, I promise you will find treasures hidden both in Hindi and Urdu whatever scripts you take up—and whatever books you take up first. You talk of the poverty of Hindi literature—you talk of the poverty of to-day's Hindi, but if you dive deep into the pages of Tulsidas, probably you share my opinion that there is no other book that stands equal to it in the literature of the world in modern languages. That one book has given me faith and hope which no other book has given. I think that it is a book which can stand any criticism and any scrutiny alike in literary grace, in metaphor and in religious fervour.

I hope also that when I come back you will have made sufficient progress in making yarn and have it woven by some village weaver for your own use. But I hope that you will be able to give sufficient proof of what wonders you have performed in spinning and I hope you will be able to share with me the same poetry and the same intellectual treat that I find in spinning if you spin with faith and hope with reference to the future of India. I hope also that your professors and teachers will give their lectures through Bengali, and I hope that, all the knowledge that you have acquired in your Government institutions, you will translate for yourselves in Bengali and that you will be able to find equivalent expressions for the richest thought that you have learnt from English poets and from English literature.

I hope also that you will approach your task with a religious faith. If this movement of ours is not religious I am free to confess to you that this movement will not only fail but it will discredit us. It is a new method of applying ourselves to the task and if we consider that we can solve the problem of India by bringing some changes only upon the old methods, we shall be doomed to disappointment. If you approach the task with the same religious fervour for which Bengal is noted, I know you will find that Swaraj is within easy reach. May God help you. May God help the professors, and may God give you the strength that our friend Srijut Chittranjandas needs. I have much pleasure in declaring this institution open.

THE DUTY OF SPINNING

In "The Secret of Swaraj" I have endeavoured to show what home-spinning means for our country. In any curriculum of the future, spinning must be a compulsory subject. Just as we cannot live without breathing and without eating, so is it impossible for us to attain economic independence and banish pauperism from this ancient land without reviving home-spinning. I hold the spinning wheel to be as much a necessity in every household as the hearth. No other scheme that can be devised will ever solve the problem of the deepening poverty of the people.

How then can spinning be introduced in every home ? I have already suggested the introduction of spinning and systematic production of yarn in every national school. Once our boys and girls have learnt the art they can easily carry it to their homes.

But this requires organisation. A spinning wheel must be worked for twelve hours per day. A practised spinner can spin two tolas and a half per hour. The price that is being paid at

present is on an average four annas per forty
tolas or one pound of yarn, *i. e.*, one pice per
hour. Each wheel therefore should give three
annas per day. A strong one costs seven rupees.
Working, therefore, at the rate of twelve hours
per day it can pay for itself in less than 38
days. I have given enough figures to work
upon. Anyone working at them will find the
results to be startling.

If every school introduced spinning, it
would revolutionize our ideas of financing
education. We can work a school for six hours
per day and give free education to the pupils.
Supposing a boy works at the wheel for four
hours daily, he will produce every day 10 tolas
of yarn and thus earn for his school one anna
per day. Suppose further that he manufactures
very little during the first month, and that the
school works only twenty-six days in the
month, He can earn after the first month Rs.
1—10 per month, A class of thirty boys would
yield, after the first month, an income of
Rs. 48-12 per month.

I have said nothing about literary training.
It can be given during the two hours out of the
six. It is easy to see that every school can be
made self-supporting without much effort and

the nation can engage experienced teachers for its schools.

The chief difficulty in working out the scheme is the spinning wheel. We require thousands of wheels if the art becomes popular. Fortunately, every village carpenter can easily construct the machine. It is a serious mistake to order them from the Ashram or any other place. The beauty of spinning is that it is incredibly simple, easily learnt, and can be cheaply introduced in every village.

The course suggested by me is intended only for this year of purification and probation. When normal times are reached and Swaraj is established one hour only may be given to spinning and the rest to literary training.

Young India—Feb. 2nd, 1921.

HAND-SPINNING AGAIN

The Servant of India has a fling too at spinning and that is based as I shall presently show an ignorance of the facts. Spinning does protect a women's virtue, because it enables women who are to-day working on public roads and are often in danger of having their modesty outraged, to protect themselves, and I know no other occupation that lacs of women can follow save spinning. Let me inform the Jesting writer that several women have already returned to the sanctity of their homes and taken to spinning which they say is the one occupation which means so such *barkat* (blessing). I claim for it the properties of a musical instrument, for whilst a hungry and a naked woman will refuse to dance to the accompaniment of a piano, I have seen women beaming with joy to see the spinning wheel work, for they know that they can through that rustic instrument both feed and clothe themselves.

Yes, it does solve the problem of India's chronic poverty and is an insurance against famine. The writer of the jests may not know the scandals that I know about irrigation and relief works. These works are largely a fraud. But if my wise counsellors will devote themselves to introducing the wheel in every home, I promise that the wheel will be an almost complete protection against famine. It is idle to cite Austria. I admit the poverty and limitations of my humanity. I can only think of India's *Kamadhenu*, and the spinning wheel is that for India. For India had the spinning wheel in every home before the advent of the East India Company. India being a cotton growing country, it must be considered a crime to import a single yard of yarn from outside. The figures quoted by the writer are irrelevant.

The fact is that inspite of the manufacture of 62-7 crores pounds of yarn in 1917-18 India imported several crore yards of foreign yarn which were woven by the mills as well as the weavers. The writer does not also seem to know that more cloth is to-day woven by our weavers than by mills, but the bulk of it is foreign yarn and therefore our weavers are supporting foreign spinners. I would not mind it much if we were doing something else instead. When spinning was almost compulsorily stopped nothing replaced it save slavery and idleness. Our mills cannot to-day spin enough for our wants, and if they did, they will not keep down prices, unless they were compelled. They are frankly Money-makers and will not therefore regulate prices according to the needs of the nations. Hand-spinning is therefore designed to put millions of rupees in the hands of poor villagers. Every agricultural country requires a supplementary industry to enable the peasants to utilise the spare hours. Such industry for India has always been spinning. Is it such a visionary ideal—an attempt to revive an ancient occupation whose destruction has brought on slavery, pauperism and disappearance of the inimitable artistic talents which was once all expressed in the wonderful fabric of India and which was the envy of the world?

And now a few figures. One boy could, if he worked say four hours daily, spin $\frac{1}{4}$ lb. of yarn. 64,000 students would, therefore, spin 16,000 lbs per day and therefore feed 8,000 weavers if a weaver wove two lbs of hand-spun yarn. But the students and others are requir-ed to spin during this year of purification by way of penance in order to popularise spinning and to add to the manufacture of hand-spun yarn so as to overtake full manufacture during the current year. The nation may be too lazy to do it. But if all put their hands to this work, it is incredibly easy, it involves very little sacrifice and saves an annual drain of sixty crores even if it does nothing else. I have discussed the matter with many mill-owners, several economists, men of business and no one has yet been able to challenge the position herein set forth. I do expect the 'Servant of India' to treat a serious subject with seriousness and accuracy of information.

Young India—Feb. 16, 1921.

HINDU MUSLIM UNITY

Mr. Gandhi, in opening the Tibbi College at Delhi on Feb. 13, said :—

Hakimji and Friends,—It was not without reluctance that I agreed to perform the ceremony of declaring this great institution formally open. I know that had it not been for the unfortunate estrangement created between the Government and ourselves his Excellency the present Viceroy would have been requested to open an institution whose foundation-stone was laid by his predecessor. You will naturally appreciate my embarrassment in finding myself a substitute for so exalted a personage as the Viceroy. The second reason for my reluctance is still more personal. I hold strange views on medicine and hospital and have scrupulously avoided any special contact with such institutions. But my reluctance was overborne by my regard for our worthy Hakimji. I must frankly confess that have undertaken to perform the ceremony for political motives. I regard the Hakimji as an embodiment of Hindu Muslim unity, without

which we can make no progress. I regard this
institution, too, as a symbol of that unity. It,
therefore, gives me pleasure to be associated
with to-day's ceremony.

You must have listened to the report
just read with interest and profit. It is
a record of substantial progress and strenu-
ous labour. It shows what one man's energy
devoted with single-mindedness can do. May
God grant long life to the Hakimji and
enable him to complete the programme
sketched by him. I hope that the monied
men of the country will lighten his labours
by sending him unsolicited donations.

You will note that, besides declaring this
institution open, I am to unveil the portraits
of Lord and Lady Hardinge. It will give me
particular pleasure to be privileged to perform
that function, giving us, as it does, an opportunity of showing that in the battle of non-co-
operation we are not actuated by an anti-
British spirit and that our national ideal
includes the treasuring of the memory of good
deeds done by anybody, be he English or
Indian.

In order to avoid any misinterpretation
of my views on medicine, I would crave your

indulgence for a few moments over a very brief
exposition of them. I have said in a booklet*
much criticised at the present moment that
the present practice of medicine is the concentrated essence of Black Magic. I believe
that a multiplicity of hospitals is no test of
civilization. It is rather a symptom of decay,
even as a multiplicity of *Pinjrapoles* is a
symptom of the indifference to the welfare of
their cattle by the people in whose midst they
are brought into being. I hope, therefore, that
this college will be concerned chiefly with the
prevention of diseases rather than their cure.
The science of sanitation is infinitely more
ennobling, though more difficult of execution,
than the science of healing. I regard the
present system as Black Magic, because it
tempts people to put an undue importance on
the body and practically ignores the spirit
within. I would urge the students and professors of the college to investigate the laws
governing the health of the spirit, and they
will find that they will yield startling results
even with reference to the cure of the body.
The present science of medicine is divorced
from religion. A man who attends to his

* "Indian Home Rule" published by Ganesh & Co., Madras.

daily *Namaz* or his *Gayatri* in the proper
spirit need never get ill. A clean spirit must
build a clean body. I am convinced that the
main rules of religious conduct conserve both
the spirit and the body. Let me hope and
pray that this college will witness a definite
attempt on the part of the physicians to bring
about a reunion between the body and the
soul. Modern medical science, having ignored
the condition of the permanent element in
the human system in diagnosing diseases, has
ignored the limitations that should naturally
exist regarding the field of its activity. In
trying to cure a body of its disease, it has
totally disregarded the claims of the sub-
human creation. Man, instead of being the
lord and, therefore, the protector of the lower
animal kingdom, has become its tyrant, and
the science of medicine has been probably his
chief instrument for tyranny. Vivisection, in
my opinion, is the blackest of all the blackest
crimes that man is at present committing
against God and his fair creation. We should
be able to refuse to live if the price of living be
the torture of sentient being. It ill becomes us
to invoke the blessings in our daily prayers of
God, the compassionate, if we in turn will not

practise elementary compassion towards our
fellow-creatures. Would to God that this
college, founded by one of the best of Indian
physicians, will bear in mind the limitations
that God, in my humble opinion, has set upon,
our activity.

Having said this much, I would like to
pay my humble tribute to the spirit of research
that fires the modern scientist. My quarrel is
not against that spirit. My complaint is
against the direction that the spirit has taken.
It has chiefly concerned itself with the
exploration of the laws and methods conduc-
ing to the merely material advancement
of its clientele. But I have nothing but
praise for the zeal, the industry and the
sacrifice that have animated the modern
scientists in their pursuit after truth. I regret
to have to record my opinion based on consider-
able experience that our Hakims and Vaids do
not exhibit that spirit in any mentionable
degree. They follow without question formulas.
They carry on little investigation. The
condition of indigenous medicine is truly
deplorable. Not having kept abreast of modern
research, their profession has fallen largely into
disrepute. I am hoping that this college will

try to remedy this grave defect and restore *Ayurvedic* and *Unani* medical science to its pristine glory. I am glad, therefore, that this institution has its western wing. Is it too much to hope that a union of the three systems will result in a harmonious blending and in purging each of special defects ?

Lastly, I shall hope this college will set its face absolutely against all quackery, western or eastern, refuse to recognise any but sterling worth, and that it will inculcate among the students the belief that the profession of medicine is not intended for earning fat fees but for alleviating pain and suffering. With the prayer that God may bless the labours of its founder and organizers, I formally declare the Tibbi College open.

THE PEACE TERMS

What will Kill Non-co-operation ?—Certainly violence on the part of non-co-operators. But that is not what I wanted to answer. What can the Government do to kill Non-co-operation ?—is the question I have been asked. A settlement of the Khilafat in accordance with the Muslim demand, a settlement of the Punjab in accordance with the Indian demand, and the grant of Swaraj in accordance with a scheme to be framed by authorised representatives of the nation.

What is Swaraj ?—That is the next question. It is partly answered in the foregoing paragraph. No one man can produce a Swaraj scheme because it is not one man's Swaraj that is wanted nor can a scheme be framed in advance. What may satisfy the nation to-day may not satisfy it to-morrow. Our evolution is and must be an organic growth. National will is therefore subject to change from day to-day. But some broad outlines can certainly be laid down in advance for any scheme of Swaraj. The nation's re-

presentatives must have full control over
education, law, police and military. We must
have full financial control. And if we are to
be self-governing not a soldier can leave
India without our consent.

What about European Interests ?—They
will be as safe in a self-governing India as
they are to-day. But there will be no privileges of a superior race, no concessions and no
exploitation. English men will live as friends
in every sense of the term but not as rulers.

And the British Connection ?—Nobody so
far as I am aware wants to end it for the sake
of ending it. There must be complete independence, if England's policy is in conflict with
the Muslim sentiment on the Khilafat question or with the Indian sentiment in the Punjab.
In any case it must be partnership at will,
based upon mutual love and esteem.

Is India Ready for this ?—Time will show,
I am convinced that it is. The Swaraj, that
the congress demands is not one that is to be
granted by England. It must be that which
the nation demands and can enforce, in the
same sense that South Africa received it.

Dhoti and Chhadar—Signs of the time
are unmistakable. A councillor in the reformed

council is reported to have appeared in dhoti
and chaddar and insisted upon taking his oath
in Bengali.   The councillor deserves congratu-
lations upon his pluck. It is the most natural
thing for us to appear in our national costume
at all functions.   And one may hope that
councillors wherever they can will co-operate
with the nation in spite of their having in
many cases flouted the nation's wish in
insisting upon going to the councils.   They
will certainly render a service if they will have
the courage to appear at Council meetings in
Khaddar dress and speak in their vernaculars.
It is easier for the few Englishmen to speak
our vernaculars than for the many of the
nation to speak English.

Young India—16th February, 1921.

THE CONDITIONS OF SWARAJ

Swaraj is easy of attainment before October next if certain simple conditions can be fulfilled. I ventured to mention one year in September last because I new that the conditions were incredibly simple and I felt that the atmosphere in the country was responsive. Past five months' experience has confirmed me in the opinion. I am convinced that the country has never been so ready for establishing Swaraj as now.

But it is necessary for us as accurately as possible to know the conditions. One supreme indispensable condition is the continuance of non-violence. Rowdyism, hooliganism, looting that we have recently witnessed are disturbing elements. They are danger-signals. We must be able to arrest their progress. The spirit of democracy cannot be established in a year in the midst of terrorism whether governmental or popular. In some respects popular terrorism is more antagonistic to the growth of the democratic spirit than the governmental. For the latter strengthens the spirit

8

of democracy, whereas the former kills it. Dyerism has evoked a yearning after freedom as nothing else has. But internal Dyerism, representing as it will terrorism by a majority, will establish an oligarchy such as will stifle the spirit of all free discussion and conduct. Non-violence, therefore, as against the Government and as between ourselves is absolutely essential to speedy success. And we must be able to devise means of observing it on our part in spite of the gravest provocations.

The next condition is our ability to bring into being the Congress organisation in terms of the new constitution, which aims at establishing a Congress agency in every village with a proper electorate. It means both money and ability to give effect to Congress policies. What is really needed is not a large measure of sacrifice but ability to organise and to take simple concerted action. At the present moment we have not even succeeded in carrying the Congress message to every home in the 7½ lacs of villages of India. To do this work means at least 250 honest workers for as many districts, who have influence in their respective districts and who believe in the Congress programme. No village, no circle need wait for instructions from head-quarters for founding their respective organisations.

There are certain things that are applicable to all. The most potent thing is Swadeshi. Every home must have the spinning wheel and every village can organise itself in less than a month and become self-supporting for its cloth. Just imagine what this silent revolution means and there would be no difficulty in sharing my belief that Swadeshi means *Swaraj* and *Swadharma.*

Every man and woman can give some money—be it even a pice—to the Tilak Swaraj Fund and we need have no anxiety about financing the movement. Every man and woman can deny himself or herself all luxury, all ornamentation, all intoxicants at least for one year. And we shall have not only money but we shall have boycotted many foreign articles. Our civilization, our culture, our Swaraj depend not upon multiplying our wants—self-indulgence, but upon restricting our wants—self-denial.

We can do nothing without Hindu-Muslim unity and without killing the snake of un-

touchability. Untouchability is a corroding
poison that is eating into the vitals of Hindu
society. *Varnashram* is not a religion of
superiority and inferiority. No man of God
can consider another man as inferior to
himself. He must consider every man as his
blood-brother. It is the cardinal principle of
every religion.

If this is a religious battle, no argument is
necessary to convince the reader that self-
denial must be its supreme test. Khilafat
cannot be saved, the Punjab humility cannot
be redressed, without godliness. Godliness
means change of heart,—in political language,
changing the angle of vision. And such a
change can come in a moment. My belief is
that India is ripe for that change.

Let us then rivet our attention on :.

(1) Cultivating the spirit of non-violence.

(2) Setting up Congress organisations in
every village.

(3) Introducing the spinning wheel in
every home and manufacturing all the cloth,
required for our wants, through the village
weaver.

(4) Collecting as much money as possible.

(5) Promoting Hindu-Muslim unity and

(6) Ridding Hinduism of the curse of untouchability and otherwise purifying ourselves by avoiding intoxicating drinks and drugs.

Have we honest, earnest, industrious, patriotic workers for this very simple programme? If we have, Swaraj will be established in India before next October.

Young India—23rd February, 1921.

'HIND SWARAJ' OR THE INDIAN HOME-RULE

It is certainly my good fortune that this booklet of mine is receiving wide attention. The original is in Gujarati. It had a chequered career. It was first published in the columns of the 'Indian Opinion' of South Africa. It was written in 1908 during my return voyage from London to South Africa in answer to the Indian school of violence, and its prototype in South Africa. I came in contact with every known Indian anarchist in London. Their bravery impressed me, but I feel that their zeal was misguided. I felt that violence was no remedy for India's ills, and that her civilization required the use of a different and higher weapon for self-protection. The *Satyagrah* of South Africa was still an infant hardly two years old. But it had developed sufficiently to permit me to write of it with some degree of confidence. It was so much appreciated that it was published as a booklet. It attracted some attention in India. The Bombay Government prohibited its circulation. I replied by publishing its translation. I thought that it was due to my English friends, that they should know its contents. In my opinion it is a book which can be put into the hands of a child. It teaches the gospel of love in the place of that of hate. It replaces violence with self-sacrifice. It pits soul force against brute force. It has gone through several editions and I commend it to those who would care to read it. I withdraw nothing except one word of it, and that in deference to a lady friend, I have given the reason for the alteration in the preface to the Indian edition.*

The booklet is a severe condemnation of 'modern civilization.' It was written in 1908. My conviction is deeper to-day than ever. I feel that if India would discard 'modern civilization,' she can only gain by doing so.

But J would warn the reader against thinking that I am to-day aiming at the Swaraj described therein. I know that India is not ripe for it. It may seem an impertinence to say so. But such is my conviction. I am individually working for the self-rule pictured therein. But to-day my corporate activity is undoubtedly devoted to the

* Published by Ganesh & Co., Madras,

attainment of Parliamentary Swaraj in accordance with the wishes of the people of India. I am not aiming at destroying railways or hospitals, though I would certainly welcome their natural destruction. Neither railways nor hospitals are a test of a high and pure civilization. At least they are a necessary evil. Neither adds one inch to the moral stature of a nation Nor am I aiming at a permanent destruction of law courts, much as I regard it as a consummation devoutly to be wished for. Still less am I trying to destroy all machinery and mills. It requires a higher simplicity and renunciation than the people are to-day prepared for.

The only part of the programme which is now being carried out in its entirety is that of non-violence. But I regret to have to confess that even that is not being carried out in the spirit of the book. If it were, India would establish Swaraj in a day. If India adopted the doctrine of love as an active part of her religion and introduced it in her politics, Swaraj would descend upon India from heaven. But I am painfully aware that that event is far off as yet.

I offer these comments because I observe
that much is being quoted from the booklet
to discredit the present movement. I have
even seen writings suggesting that I am
playing a deep game, that I am using the
present turmoil to foist my fads on India,
and am making religious experiments at
India's expense. I can only answer that
Satyagrah is made of sterner stuff. There is
nothing reserved and nothing secret in it. A
portion of the whole theory of life described
in 'Hind Swaraj' is undoubtedly being carried
into practice. There is no danger attendant
upon the whole of it being practised. But it
is not right to scare away people by reproduc-
ing from my writings passages that are irrelevant to the issue before the country.

Young India—26th January, 1921.